# THIRTY-SIX CHANSONS
# BY FRENCH PROVINCIAL COMPOSERS
## (1529–1550)

# RECENT RESEARCHES IN THE MUSIC OF THE RENAISSANCE

*James Haar and Howard Mayer Brown, general editors*

---

A-R Editions, Inc., publishes six quarterly series—

*Recent Researches in the Music of the Middle Ages and Early Renaissance,*
Margaret Bent, general editor;

*Recent Researches in the Music of the Renaissance,*
James Haar and Howard Mayer Brown, general editors;

*Recent Researches in the Music of the Baroque Era,*
Robert L. Marshall, general editor;

*Recent Researches in the Music of the Classical Era,*
Eugene K. Wolf, general editor;

*Recent Researches in the Music of the Nineteenth and Early Twentieth Centuries,*
Jerald C. Graue, general editor;

*Recent Researches in American Music,*
H. Wiley Hitchcock, general editor—

which make public music that is being brought to light
in the course of current musicological research.

Each volume in the *Recent Researches* is devoted
to works by a single composer or to a single genre of composition,
chosen because of its potential interest to scholars and performers,
and prepared for publication according to the standards that govern
the making of all reliable historical editions.

Correspondence should be addressed:

A-R EDITIONS, INC.
315 West Gorham Street
Madison, Wisconsin 53703

RECENT RESEARCHES IN THE MUSIC OF THE RENAISSANCE • VOLUME XXXVIII

# THIRTY-SIX CHANSONS BY FRENCH PROVINCIAL COMPOSERS (1529–1550)

Edited by Leta E. Miller

A-R EDITIONS, INC. • MADISON

ISSN 0486-123X

ISBN 0-89579-157-9

Library of Congress Cataloging in Publication Data:
Thirty-six chansons.

  (Recent researches in the music of the
Renaissance , ISSN 0486-123X ; v. 38)
   For 4-5 voices.
   1. Chansons, Polyphonic.   I. Miller, Leta E.
II. Series.
M2.R2384        vol. 38        [M1579]        81-14886
ISBN 0-89579-157-9                        AACR2

# Contents

# Preface

## Introduction

The advent of single-impression printing contributed heavily to the popularity of the chanson during the second quarter of the sixteenth century. A wealth of chansonniers were issued during this time, not only in Paris, where Pierre Attaingnant published more than sixty collections containing the works of approximately 140 composers, but also by such printers as Moderne in Lyons, Susato in Antwerp, and Gardano in Venice.

Traditionally, this vast body of literature has been divided into two broad categories—chansons in the French, or "Parisian" style (which, in spite of its name, includes works by composers from the French provinces as well as from Paris), and chansons in the Flemish style. However, as Lawrence Bernstein has shown,[1] the term "Parisian chanson" may in fact be too all-encompassing; two recent studies[2] suggest substantial stylistic reasons for subdividing the French group of composers into the Parisians and their contemporaries in the provinces, who were separated from the cultural mainstream.

Since a large number of works by Parisian composers are already available in transcription, the present edition aims at expanding the basis for study of four- and five-voice chansons published between 1529 and 1550 by focusing entirely on compositions of the provincial masters.[3] This collection includes works by seventeen composers who resided for substantial periods in provincial cities.[4] While all of these masters are represented to some degree in the publications of Attaingnant, many of their works survive exclusively in the chansonniers of Jacques Moderne. Indeed, the latter's *Parangon des Chansons*[5] provided lively competition for Attaingnant and added a sizable body of works to the literature. After mid-century, chansons of the same type as found in the Attaingnant and Moderne collections continued to be published by Nicolas Du Chemin, Le Roy et Ballard, Pierre Phalèse, et al. One work in the present edition, Pierre Colin's *Comment, mon coeur*, is taken from a Du Chemin print.

## The Composers

Most of the seventeen composers represented in this edition were employed by churches, either as choirmasters or as organists (see Table 1). Biographical information for several of them is derived from the title pages of their published works. Pierre Cadéac, for example, is identified as "Master of the Choirboys at Auch" in his *Missa Alma Redemptoris* (Du Chemin, 1556); Pierre Colin's position as "*maître des enfants*" in Autun is mentioned in publications from 1550 through 1556; and the title page of Nicolas de Marle's *Missa . . . O gente brunette* (1568) provides the only information on this composer's occupation—director of the choirboys at Noyon.[6] Both Cadéac and Colin apparently took up residence in their respective cities at an earlier date than is indicated by these publications. Indirect evidence suggests that Colin lived in Autun as early as 1539, and Cadéac is mentioned in a poem about Auch that was published in 1551.[7]

Other composers are identified through citations in historical studies and documents. For example, G. Desjardins, in his monograph on the Cathedral at Beauvais, mentioned Jean Doublet (organist from 1532 to ca. 1540), Robert Godard (Doublet's successor), and Nicolle des Celliers d'Hesdin (director of the choirboys during the 1530s).[8] Hesdin, who may have been Godard's teacher, died in Beauvais on 21 August 1538.

In a study of the *maîtrise* at Rouen, A. R. Collette and A. Bourdon referred to François Dulot as *maître de chapelle* from 1523 through 1531.[9] (The composer's three extant printed chansons all appeared around 1530.) Although Dulot seemingly had a good reputation as a composer, he was not overly conscientious in fulfilling his church duties. The cathedral chapter reproached him several times regarding the management and direction of his students, as the following quotation shows:

> There were complaints that they were not adequately trained, . . . that they carried out their duties poorly, not knowing the ceremonies well, . . . that they lacked gravity and reserve in the choir, . . . that they went out of the *maîtrise* without permission in order to go to town to recite comedies. . . .[10]

Dulot also served as master of the choirboys in Amiens in 1514.[11]

J.-A. Clerval's study of *L'ancienne maîtrise de Notre-Dame de Chartres* documents the life of Jean

## Table 1. Biographical information for the seventeen provincial composers.

| Composer | City of residence | Type of employment | Extant à 4 and à 5 printed chansons |
|---|---|---|---|
| Bastard, Jean | Bourges | Master of choirboys | 2 |
| Cadéac, Pierre | Auch | Master of choirboys | 9 & 3? * |
| Colin, Pierre | Autun | Master of choirboys; organist | 7 |
| Coste, Gabriel | Lyons | ? | 16 |
| Doublet, Jean | Beauvais | Organist | 2 |
| Dulot, François | Amiens Rouen | Master of choirboys *Maître de chapelle* | 2 & 1? |
| Fresneau, Henry | Lyons | ? | 21 & 4? * |
| Godard, Robert | Beauvais | Organist | 13 & 4? * |
| Guyon, Jean | Chartres | Master of choirboys | 16 & 1? * |
| Hesdin, Nicolle des Celliers d' | Beauvais | Master of choirboys | 8 |
| Le Bouteiller, Jean | Bourges and Chartres | Master of choirboys | 4 |
| Le Heurteur, Guillaume | Tours | Preceptor of choirboys | 14 & 2? * |
| Marle, Nicolas de | Noyon | Master of choirboys | 12 |
| Morel, Clément | Nevers | Master of choirboys | 18 |
| Samin, Vulfran | Amiens | *"Chantre extraordinaire"* | 16 |
| Senterre, Pierre | Poitiers | Organist | 7 & 2? * |
| Villiers, Pierre de | Lyons | ?Music teacher at *Collège de la Trinité*; ?editor for Moderne | 46 & 3? * |

* Of the works with multiple attributions among the sources, one is given to Cadéac and Le Heurteur, two to Fresneau and Senterre, one to Fresneau and Guyon, and one to Godard and Villiers.

Guyon, who was registered as an *enfant de choeur* at the cathedral in 1523, directed the *maîtrise* from ca. 1541 until ca. 1556, was appointed a canon there in 1545, and celebrated his sixtieth birthday in the city in 1574.[12] Also mentioned by Clerval is Jean Le Bouteiller, who preceded Guyon as *maître* at Chartres. Le Bouteiller assumed this position in 1535, after having served as master of the boys' choir of Ste.-Chapelle in Bourges from November 1530.[13] After he moved to Chartres, his position at Bourges was assumed by Jean Bastard, who remained in the city until 1552.

For biographical information on Bastard, as well as on several other provincial composers, we rely on archival research by François Lesure, whose findings were published in a brief article, "Some Minor French Composers of the Sixteenth Century."[14] Lesure has documented the residences and occupations of Vulfran Samin, *"chantre extraordinaire de la confrérie Notre-Dame du Puy d'Amiens"* in 1543-4; Pierre Senterre, organist at the cathedral in Poitiers during the 1550s (but probably resident there much earlier); and Clément Morel, master of the boys' choir at Nevers.[15] (We know that in 1552,

Ste.-Chapelle in Bourges offered Morel the position just vacated by Bastard.) Guillaume Le Heurteur, whose chansons were published by Attaingnant, Moderne, Du Chemin, and Gardano, served as canon and preceptor of the choirboys at St.-Martin in Tours from 1545.[16]

Particularly difficult biographical problems are posed in connection with the three masters from Lyons—Gabriel Coste, Henry Fresneau, and Pierre de Villiers—all of whom have been linked to the city by strong, but totally circumstantial, evidence.[17] In the case of Fresneau, seventeen of the twenty-one chansons definitely attributable to him were published by Jacques Moderne; only one of these seventeen was also issued elsewhere.[18] Moderne must certainly have been attracted by the works of this little-known master, since half of the pieces in his collection *Le Difficile des Chansons, second Livre . . .* (1544) are by Fresneau. Furthermore, three of the composer's chanson texts appear to allude to Lyons.[19]

Like Fresneau, Gabriel Coste had close ties to Moderne. Eighteen of his nineteen known compositions survive exclusively in Moderne's editions. Furthermore, the only reference to the composer's first name comes from Moderne's collection of *ricercari* and dances *Musique de Joye* (published ca. 1544),[20] the last piece of which is ascribed to "Gabriel Costa."[21]

In the case of Pierre de Villiers, there is a similar dearth of biographical information in spite of the large corpus of extant works. It seems apparent, however, that he must have lived in Lyons for a substantial period of time for the following reasons: (1) in Moderne's *Parangon des Chansons*, the works of Villiers are found more frequently than those of any other composer;[22] (2) his chanson *Lo meissony* is in the dialect of Lyons;[23] (3) Barthélemy Aneau, principal of the *Collège de la Trinité* in Lyons, used Villiers' *Le dueil issu* as the model for his *noël, Le jour issu;*[24] and (4) the *Lyonnais* poet Charles de Sainte-Marthe dedicated a work to "Villiers, *musicien tres perfaict*" in his *Poésie Françoise* of 1540.[25] (Villiers, in turn, selected two other poems from this same literary collection for use as chanson texts.) On the basis of this information, at least two scholars have speculated on Villiers' possible occupation in Lyons. Frank Dobbins suggests that he "might have been employed to teach music at the *Collège de la Trinité,*" while Samuel Pogue proposes that he may have served Moderne as an editor for the *Parangon* series.[26]

The vast majority of chansons by these seventeen composers were published between the years 1529 and 1550 by Attaingnant or Moderne. However, a small number of their works (16 out of a total of over 200)[27] appeared after mid-century; this group of later works is included neither in the present edition, nor in the stylistic analysis presented below. Table 2 gives the dates of initial publication for all of the extant printed four- and five-voice chansons of each composer.

---

**Table 2. Dates of initial publication of the chansons of the seventeen provincial composers.** (Reprints and questionable works not included).

| | |
|---|---|
| Dulot, François | 1529-32 |
| Hesdin, Nicolle des Celliers d' | 1529-38 |
| Le Heurteur, Guillaume | 1530-41 |
| Le Bouteiller, Jean | 1532-40 |
| Guyon, Jean | 1533-50 |
| Cadéac, Pierre | 1534-41 |
| Morel, Clément | 1534-57 |
| Doublet, Jean | 1536 |
| Senterre, Pierre | 1536-57 |
| Villiers, Pierre de | 1536-59 |
| Godard, Robert | 1536-61 |
| Coste, Gabriel | 1538-43 |
| Colin, Pierre | 1538-50 |
| Fresneau, Henry | 1538-54 |
| Marle, Nicolas de | 1544-54 |
| Samin, Vulfran | 1546-59 |
| Bastard, Jean | 1547-50 |

---

## The Provincial Chansons Compared to Those of Leading Parisian Composers

A recent study of the chansons of these and other composers from the French provinces[28] has revealed several significant differences between their works and those of leading Parisian masters. In a statistical comparison using 136 chansons by provincial composers and a comparable number by such Parisians as Sermisy and Certon,[29] marked differences were discovered in four areas.

1. The provincial works display a greater amount of musical extension through text repetition. In the sample of provincial chansons, over 90% of the settings of short poems and 48% of the settings of long poems show significant amounts of text repetition;

in the Parisian sample, on the other hand, only about 36% of the works in both categories can be so characterized.

2. One-third of the provincial chansons considered in the study contain instances of "word-painting," while less than a quarter of the Parisian works use this device.

3. In general, the provincial chansons contain fewer homorhythmic passages than do the Parisian works, although the texture of the provincial chanson changed significantly during the twenty-year period under consideration (see below).

4. Nearly half of the provincial chansons studied contain internal melodic relationships, while only 14% of the Parisian works show this trait.

Whether these differences are the result of geographic diversity or whether they merely reflect the training and aesthetic preferences of the individual composers cannot be positively ascertained. However, the more complex texture of many of the provincial works suggests that the influence of the Franco-Flemish tradition may have been stronger in the provinces than in Paris.

On the other hand, the provincial and Parisian chansons show significant similarities in several areas: (1) both use the same types of texts; (2) cadences generally mark the ends of poetic lines in both types; (3) the most popular modes in both provincial and Parisian chansons are G Dorian and F "new" Lydian (i.e., with a B-flat), these modes being strongly reinforced through cadence points and imitative entries; (4) the chanson rhythm ♩♪♪ appears frequently in both types, while triple meter is rare; and (5) both the provincial and the Parisian composers made frequent use of a tripartite musical form (see below).

In addition to their value as a source of comparison with Parisian works, the provincial chansons collected herein are worthy of study in their own right. The compositions have been selected to reflect accurately both chronological trends and general stylistic traits of the provincial chanson literature published between 1529 and 1550. While the edition includes works by as great a variety of composers as possible, the number of pieces by each master is roughly proportional to his total output.

## The Style of the Provincial Chansons

*The Poetic Texts and Their Relation to the Musical Settings*

The poems used for both the Parisian and the provincial chansons generally contain lines of equal length—most frequently of ten syllables. These decasyllabic texts are usually serious, dealing with the traditional *amour courtoise* and emphasizing the grief of unrequited love (e.g., *Tristesse, ennuy* by Villiers, p. 86). Poems with shorter lines (eight syllables being most common) occur less frequently and tend to be lighter in nature; these texts are often narrative, with subjects ranging from the pastoral to the obscene. (For examples of the latter, see Guyon's *Gaultier rancontra*, p. 33, or Marle's *Frere Jehan*, p. 52.)

The decasyllabic verse almost invariably contains a clear caesura after the fourth syllable of each line; this caesura tends to be reflected in the musical setting by a long note, a melisma, or a rest. Comparison of the chansons of Parisian and provincial composers revealed that the latter were often more literal in their settings; that is, they more frequently tended to use an actual rest at the caesura in the text.

The style of the music appears to be directly related to the subjects and line-lengths of the poetry. The lighter poems are generally set in a "patter" style that features a syllabic text setting and predominantly short note values. For the serious texts, on the other hand, a "lyric" style, using longer notes and frequent melismas, is far more common.

The total number of lines within the poem may vary, the most common forms being the *quatrain*, *cinquain*, *huitain*, and *dizain*. As Lawrence Bernstein has shown, the shorter texts are more common in the chanson prints of the 1530s, while eight- and ten-line poems are found more frequently in chansons of the 1540s.[30]

Repetition of short text segments within a work is usually indicated in the original prints by the sign *ij*. In ten-syllable poems, this sign most often refers to the part of the text line that is set off by the caesura (i.e., approximately half a line); internal evidence, including melodic correspondences between phrases, the number of notes above the *ij* sign, and variants among different editions of the same piece, favors this interpretation. Less often, text repetition is written out, in which case it frequently involves more or less than half a line.

While the provincial composers often emphasized the structure of the verse by marking the caesura with a rest and the end of a poetic line with a cadence, they also used musical devices to highlight the meaning of individual words or phrases. This kind of emphasis is most often brought about through such rhythmic means as sudden long notes on "Helas" (see *Thenot estoit*, m. 29) or "O cueur lassif" (see Colin's *Comment, mon coeur*, mm. 33 ff., and Vulfran's *Comment, mon cueur*, mm. 22 ff.). Among the more unusual examples of illustrative rhythms are those in Fresneau's *Souspir d'amours*, where the composer uses short rests between repetitions of the opening two words to create a musical "sigh," and in Guyon's *Gaultier rancontra*, in which the persistent dotted rhythm on the words "faiz le moy" portrays an excited lover literally panting in eagerness. (See *Souspir d'amours*, mm. 1-5, and *Gaultier rancontra*, mm. 35-45.) While this "word-painting" in no way equals, either in means or frequency, the ingenuity of word-painting in the later Italian madrigal, it does occur more often in the provincial works than in those by leading Parisian composers.

## Musical Texture

Although the chanson of this period has often been described as primarily homorhythmic in nature,[31] most of the provincial works contain few chordal passages. Their texture is generally contrapuntal—both imitative and non-imitative—though short homorhythmic sections that frequently highlight important or dramatic texts (e.g., Villiers' *Le dueil issu*, mm. 10-12) are interspersed throughout these works.

The imitative writing is quite simple, often involving only the first three or four notes of each entry; moreover, these first notes frequently include several repeated tones, as in Le Heurteur's *Ma dame ung jour* (mm. 4 ff. and 11 ff.). Non-imitative polyphony is also common, particularly in the works of Pierre de Villiers. In fact, Villiers' compositions are often quite intricate; many display long, interweaving melodic lines and complex contrapuntal writing. An example of such complexity is Villiers' chanson *Elle est m'amye*, a five-voice work, the upper two parts of which are in canon at the unison. Only four voice-parts of this chanson are notated, the fifth being indicated by the rather cryptic instruction, "Qui suyvre me vouldra deux pauses en souspirant pausera," indicating that the canonic voice must wait two *pauses* (semibreve-rests) and two *soupirs* (semiminim-rests)[32] before entering (see Plate I). In a transcription with note values halved, the *comes* thus enters five beats after the *dux*, a fact that inevitably alters the points of harmonic stress. In mm. 10-11, for example, the final note of the phrase is rhythmically weak in the *dux*, but a point of cadential resolution in the *comes*.

Interestingly, the texture of the provincial chanson became increasingly homorhythmic during the twenty-year period under consideration, possibly as a result of the influence of the simpler, more chordal Parisian style. Chordal passages occur with greater frequency in the later works. In the sample of provincial chansons selected for the study mentioned above, nearly 80% of those published between 1529 and 1536 contain little or no homorhythm. Among those published between 1543 and 1550, however, only 24% can be so characterized. (Comparable percentages for the Parisian sample are 33% in the 1529 to 1536 period and 12.5% in the years between 1543 and 1550.) Bastard's *Soyez seur*, published in 1547, is among the rare provincial works that are almost entirely chordal.

## Melody and Rhythm

The contour of the melodic line in the upper voice is generally conjunct; leaps of more than a fifth are rare (although not absent). A cursory examination of the chansons reveals a high proportion of repeated notes. However, the prevalence of these repeated tones may be merely a result of subdividing larger rhythmic units; indeed, the harmonic rhythm generally moves on the level of the semibreve, while the repeated notes are most often found in minim passages.

The majority of chansons are set in duple mensuration throughout. When triple mensuration does occur, it appears most frequently in the middle of a work and almost always in a homorhythmic passage.

The conventional "chanson rhythm" (see above) is a common, but by no means universal, opening. Its frequent occurrence is obviously the result of the metric structure of the text: the decasyllabic line, with its strong caesura after the fourth syllable, often logically generates the rhythmic sequence $-\,\cup\,\cup\,-$, as in the following example:

$$- \quad \cup \quad \cup \quad -$$

Oeil importum / qui mon cueur a rendu (Fresneau)

Thus, once again, internal evidence suggests that the chanson composers were strongly influenced by the metric qualities of the poetic line.

## Musical Form

The musical form of the chanson is closely linked to the structure of the text: a line of poetry often corresponds to a musical phrase marked by a cadence. At the same time, however, the majority of chansons studied—both those by provincial composers and those by Parisians—display a larger, tripartite structure delineated by the pattern of musical repetition. Sectional repeats may occur at two points within the form: at the beginning and at the close. The latter, by far the more common of the two, functions to provide a substantial and coherent ending to a work; almost all of the chansons of this period conclude this way. The music in such repeats is always sung with the same words (either one or two poetic lines, depending on the length of the text), and the beginning of the section is marked in the original prints by the sign 𝄋,. Repetition of the first section, however, serves a different function: here, it appears to be solely a means of accommodating extra poetic lines. It is used only in settings of longer poems (eight and ten lines), and it always involves a change of text upon repetition of the music. Generally, in such first-section repeats, four poetic lines are involved, two for each rendition of the music. The point of repetition is indicated in the original prints by a repeat sign placed on the staff.

These two sections—the first and the last—may contain either the same or different musical material. Between them lies a central unrepeated passage. Thus, four possible forms are generated from the combination of these factors (see Table 3). In four- and eight-line text settings, the central "b" section contains only two poetic lines; with five- and ten-line texts, however, the central section is expanded to accommodate the extra literary material.

This tripartite form is often strengthened by complementary structural factors. For example, in Pierre de Villiers' *Autant que moy* (see p. 69), each section begins with the same type of melodic figure. The downward leap at the opening of the chanson is recalled by a tonal inversion in measure 28 (section "b"). In measure 42 (section "C"), a link to the opening of the chanson is again formed, not only by the upward leap of the fourth, but also by an inversion of the scale first presented in measure 2. Finally, the last line of text is also set to a similar motive containing the scale passage but not the opening leap. Thus Villiers creates an aural link between significant structural points, while avoiding the monotony of direct repetition.

Furthermore, an examination of the cadential tones within this chanson reveals a careful plan (see Table 4). Sections "C" and "a" contain opposite cadential structures; this is coupled with the reverse melodic movement described above. Section "b" contains only Phrygian or weak internal cadences.

To avoid the problems inherent in large amounts of musical repetition, the second statement of a section is sometimes varied. Guyon's *De noz deux cueurs*, a *cinquain* set in the form a b ‖A‖, would be more accurately diagrammed a b A' A". Marle's *Frere Jehan* contains an alteration of both the "a" and "C" sections (a a' b C C').

In some chansons, the correlation between text length and musical form appears to be very specific.

---

**Table 3. Tripartite musical forms used in the chansons**

|  | First and last sections different | | First and last sections same | |
|---|---|---|---|---|
| **No repetition of first section** | 1. (music:)   a    b    ‖C‖ <br> (text lines:)   1    2-3    4 <br> or <br> 1    2-4    5 | | 2.   a    b    ‖A‖ <br> 1    2-3    4 <br> or <br> 1    2-4    5 | |
| **With repetition of first section** | 3. (music:) a   a   b   ‖C‖ <br> (text lines:) 1-2   3-4   5-6   7-8 <br> or <br> 1-2   3-4   5-8   9-10 | | 4.   a   a   b   ‖A‖ <br> 1-2   3-4   5-6   7-8 <br> or <br> 1-2   3-4   5-8   9-10 | |

(Capital letters indicate repetition of both words and music; small letters indicate identical music with new text.)

## Table 4. Cadence points in *Autant que moy*

| Sections: | a    a | b | ‖: C :‖ |
|---|---|---|---|
| Cadence tones: | D  (mm. 7 & 20)<br><br>A (mm. 14 & 27) | E (Phrygian; m. 32)<br>D (weak; m. 36)<br>D (weak; m. 38)<br>D (m. 41) | A (mm. 47 & 58)<br><br>D (mm. 53 & 65) |

(Repeats of sections "a" and "C" are written out.)

In the works of the provincial composers, the five-line poems are found most often in form 2 (a b ‖A:‖), the eight-line poems in form 3 (a a b ‖C:‖), and the ten-line poems in form 4 (a a b ‖A:‖).[33] These correspondences are probably a result of both the amount of repetition within the various structures and the length of the central "b" section. Obviously, forms 2 and 4 contain less variety than forms 1 and 3, since, in form 2, the "a" section is heard three times, and in form 4, it is heard four times. In four- and eight-line texts, where the "b" section includes only two poetic lines, the use of form 2 or 4 would result in almost the entire work consisting of "A." In five- or ten-line texts, on the other hand, there is more intermediary material in "b," and thus the recurrence of "A" may in fact be desirable as a unifying device. Although this tripartite structure is used consistently by composers in both Paris and the provinces, it should be noted that the early chansons of Clément Janequin stand as important exceptions. These works are often organized by means other than the stereotyped structures detailed above.[34]

The formal analysis of tripartite structure is, of necessity, a generalized description of the chanson repertoire. Nevertheless, such generalizations often prove to be valuable frameworks from which to view minor divergencies and individual variations. The discussion of tripartite division is presented here as a general analytic tool that is based on a broad view of the chanson form of this period.

## Sources

The chansonniers of Pierre Attaingnant and Jacques Moderne are the primary sources for the current transcriptions. In most cases, the latest publication of a particular work by one of these two printers was selected as the main source,[35] since these later revisions often corrected obvious errors or awkward passages in the earlier editions. However, variant readings from the earlier sources are cited in the Critical Notes below.

Although the chanson repertoires in the publications of Attaingnant and Moderne contain frequent duplications, it is not always possible to substantiate outright plagiarism on the part of one printer or the other. In fact, the conflicting composer attributions and variant musical readings found in many of these concordances suggest that at least part of the material was obtained from different sources by each of the two publishers.[36]

Listed below in Table 5 are the printed editions that are sources of the chansons contained in this volume, with an indication (*) of the primary source used for each transcription. The numerical designations include RISM numbers and reference numbers from the appropriate bibliographic catalogues (see below). Abbreviations refer to these catalogues as follows:

(1) *H.*: Heartz, Daniel. *Pierre Attaingnant, Royal Printer of Music: A Historical Study and Bibliographical Catalogue.* Berkeley and Los Angeles: University of California Press, 1969.

(2) *P.*: Pogue, Samuel F. *Jacques Moderne.* Geneva: Librairie Droz, 1969.

(3) *L-Th.*: Lesure, F., and Thibault, G. "Bibliographie des éditions musicales publiées par Nicolas du Chemin (1549-1576)." *Annales Musicologiques* I: 269-373.

(4) *L-Th.*: Idem, *Bibliographie des éditions d'Adrian Le Roy et Robert Ballard.* Paris: Société française de musicologie, 1955.

## Editorial Procedures

Note values are halved in transcription. The sign ₵, which appears at the beginning of all of the

**Table 5.**

| Composer | Chanson | Sources |
|---|---|---|
| Bastard | *Soyez seur* | Attaingnant: 1547[12] (*H.* 149)* |
| Cadéac | *Amour et moy* | Attaingnant: 1541[6] (*H.* 99); 1541[5] (*H.* 100)* |
| | *En languissant* | Attaingnant: 1538[12] (*H.* 82); 1540[10] (*H.* 95)* |
| | | Moderne: 1538[17] (*P.* 13) |
| Colin | *Comment, mon coeur* | Du Chemin: 1550[12] (*L-Th.* 13)* |
| Coste | *Si les oyseaulx* | Moderne: 1539[20] (*P.* 21)* |
| | *Ung pouvre aymant* | Moderne: 1539[20] (*P.* 21)* |
| Doublet | *Combien que j'ay* | Attaingnant: 1536[5] (*H.* 72)* |
| Dulot | *En esperant* | Attaingnant: 1529[2] (*H.* 14)* |
| Fresneau | *Mignons qui suivés* | Moderne: 1539[20] (*P.* 21)* |
| | *Oeil importum* | Attaingnant: 1547[8] (*H.* 144)* |
| | *Souspir d'amours* | Moderne: 1539[20] (*P.* 21)* |
| | *Thenot estoit* | See listing under "Senterre or Fresneau." |
| Godard | *Longtemps y a* | Attaingnant: 1543[8] (*H.* 109); 1543[7] (*H.* 110); 1550[6] (*H.* 163)* |
| | *Mariez-moy* | Attaingnant: 1538[12] (*H.* 82); 1540[10] (*H.* 95)* |
| Guyon | *De noz deux cueurs* | Attaingnant: *H.* 41; 1536[3] (*H.* 71)* |
| | *Gaultier rancontra* | Attaingnant: 1545[10] (*H.* 126); 1545[11] (*H.* 127)* |
| Hesdin | *Doeul, double doeul* | Attaingnant: 1530[4] (*H.* 19); 1536[3] (*H.* 71); 1537[3] (*H.* 76); 1537[3] (*H.* 78)* |
| | | Le Roy/Ballard: 1561[7]; 1567[12] (*L-Th.* 129); 1573[14] (*L-Th.*183) |
| | | Susato: 1544[10] (attr. to Lupi) |
| Le Bouteiller | *Ce moys de may* | Attaingnant: 1540[14] (*H.* 92); 1542[13] (*H.* 106)* |
| Le Heurteur | *Ma dame ung jour* | Attaingnant: 1534[14] (*H.* 54); 1537[4] (*H.* 79)* |
| | *Or my rendez* | Attaingnant: 1530[3] (*H.*18)* |
| | *Souvent amour* | Attaingnant: *H.* 41; 1536[3] (*H.* 71); 1537[3] (*H.* 76); 1537[3] (*H.* 78)* |
| | | Du Chemin: 1551[7] (*L-Th.* 22) |
| Marle | *Frere Jehan* | Attaingnant: 1550[5] (*H.* 160)* |
| | *L'enfant Amour* | Attaingnant: *H.* 116; 1544[7] (*H.* 117); 1544[8] (*H.* 118)* |

chansons in the sources, is retained in the modern notation. Time-signature changes on the staff are generally editorial. Triple mensuration is indicated in the sources by a "3" placed on the staff, and the return to duple meter by the sign ₵. These indications have been rendered in the transcription by [$\frac{3}{2}$] followed by [₵] or [$\frac{2}{4}$].

Spellings are left as in the original prints, except that: (1) "i" used as a consonant is changed to "j," and "v" used as a vowel is now "u"; and (2) the *accent aigu* has been added when it is required for clarification of the text. Punctuation has been added for text clarification. The composers' names are spelled as they appear in the primary source for each transcription. The author of the text, when known, is cited at the head of each piece, in the upper left corner.

In the underlay of the text, brackets ([ ]) are used for repetitions that are indicated in the original print by *ij*; angled brackets ( < > ) surround editorial additions of text.

Accidentals above the staff are editorial; optional or debatable ones are in brackets; cautionary accidentals are in parentheses. A continuous overhead bracket ( ⌐⌐ ) indicates a ligature, a broken overhead bracket ( ⌐ ⌐ ) indicates coloration, and the symbol ∮ appears at those points where it occurred in the original sources.

## Critical Notes

The editorial notes below include both documentation of variant readings from supplementary sources and citations of obvious errors in the pri-

| Composer | Chanson | Sources |
|---|---|---|
| Morel | Est-il possible | Attaingnant: 1536[5] (H. 72); 1538[11] (H. 81); 1540[9] (H. 94); 1549[17] (H. 161)* |
| | | Du Chemin: 1551[4] (L-Th. 19) |
| | Plaisir n'ay plus | Attaingnant: 1540[11] (H. 96)* |
| Samin | Amour m'a mis | Attaingnant: 1548[4] (H. 151)* |
| | Comment, mon cueur | Attaingnant: 1546[14] (H. 137)* |
| Senterre | Faict-elle pas bien | Attaingnant: 1536[4] (H. 69); 1538[10] (H. 80); 1546[11] (H. 140)* |
| Senterre or | | |
| Fresneau | Thenot estoit | Moderne: 1544[9] (P. 40) Fresneau |
| | | Attaingnant: 1545[10] (H. 126); 1545[11] (H. 127)* Senserre |
| | | Du Chemin: 1549[28] (L-Th. 6); 1551[6] (L-Th. 21) Santerre |
| Villiers | Autant que moy | Attaingnant: 1540[12] (H. 97)* |
| | Cueur sans mercy | Moderne: 1538[16] (P. 12) |
| | | Attaingnant: 1540[10] (H. 95)* |
| | Elle est m'amye | Moderne: 1538[16] (P. 12)* |
| | En grant douleur | Attaingnant: 1538[12] (H. 82); 1540[10] (H. 95)* |
| | | Moderne: 1538[15] (P. 11) |
| | Est-il ung mal | Attaingnant: 1540[13] (H. 89) |
| | | Moderne: 1541[7] (P. 30)* |
| | Le dueil issu | Moderne: 1538[17] (P. 13)* |
| | | Attaingnant: 1540[9] (H. 94); 1549[17] (H. 161) |
| | | Du Chemin: 1551[4] (L-Th. 19) |
| | Rien n'est plus cher | Attaingnant: 1543[12] (H. 113); H. 113 bis.; 1543[11] (H. 114); 1549[18] (H. 159)* |
| | | Du Chemin: 1549[28] (L-Th. 6); 1551[6] (L-Th. 21); L-Th. 85 |
| | | Le Roy/Ballard: 1564[12] (L-Th. 91) |
| | Tristesse, ennuy | Moderne: 1539[20] (P. 21) |
| | | Attaingnant: 1540[11] (H. 96)* |

mary source that have been corrected in the present edition. References are identified by composer, short title, measure number, and voice part (S, Ct, T, and B for Superius, Contratenor, Tenor, and Bassus). The following abbreviations for note values are used: Br = Breve; SB = Semibreve; Mi = Minim; SM = Semiminim; F = Fusa. Variants are listed by RISM number (see section on Sources). Pitch notation uses c′ for middle c. For voice parts notated with an 8 beneath the treble clef, octave notation in the Critical Notes refers to the sounding pitch, not the notated pitch. Unless otherwise indicated, all descriptions refer to the primary source for each piece (see p. xiii).

Bastard, *Soyez seur*
M. 4, T, note 1 is a dotted SB; note 2 has been substituted for the dot to accommodate the text accents and to correspond to the repetition of the same music in mm. 12 and 33. M. 31, note 2-m. 32, note 1, Ct, tie omitted; added here by analogy with T and B in these mm.

Cadéac, *Amour et moy*
M. 2, T, rest is a Br-rest; changed here by analogy with mm. 21-22. Mm. 18-21, Ct reads as follows in 1541[5]: c′ (Mi), d′ (SB), g′ (dotted SB), g′ (Mi), g′ (Mi), f′ (Mi), g′ (SB), e′ (SB), e′ (SB), c′ (Mi).

Cadéac, *En languissant*
M. 15, S, note 1 is a Br and the rest is omitted in 1538[17]. M. 24, Ct, beat 4 comprised of SM (f′) and 2 F's (e′, d′) in 1538[17].

Doublet, *Combien que j'ay*
M. 21, S, dot following note 4 (represented here by the tie to m. 22) is missing.

Dulot, *En esperant*

This chanson is also transcribed in Henry Expert, ed., *Maîtres musiciens de la renaissance française* (Paris: Leduc, 1897), vol. 5: 36-39. M. 6, B, note 3 has no dot and notes 4 and 5 are SM's; changed here by analogy with m. 29. M. 29, S, note 1 is dotted and notes 2 and 3 are F's; changed here by analogy with m. 6.

Fresneau, *Mignons*

M. 28, Ct, note 5 is a'. M. 31, S, note 6 is a Mi.

Guyon, *Gaultier*

M. 2, Ct, note 3 is omitted; added here by analogy with mm. 12-13.

Hesdin, *Doeul*

This chanson is also transcribed in Friedrich Blume, ed., *Das Chorwerk* (Wolfenbüttel, 1931), vol. 15, with an attribution to J. Lupi. M. 13, T, note 2 is an a in 1544[10]. M. 15, Ct, note 2 is a dotted Mi and note 3 is a SM (g?) in 1530[4]. M. 16, Ct, a single SB appears in place of notes 3 and 4; transcription here follows the reading in 1530[4] and 1544[10]. M. 19, B, note 1 is an A in 1544[10]. M. 22, Ct reads dotted SB (e'), Mi (e') in 1544[10]. M. 23, Ct, note 3 is a dotted SB, and the rest at the beginning of m. 24 is omitted in 1544[10]. M. 24, Ct, last note is replaced by 2 SM's (g', e') in 1544[10]. M. 32, S, note 1 replaced by SB and SB-rest in 1544[10]. M. 40, Ct, note 1 is an e' in 1544[10].

Le Heurteur, *Or my rendez*

M. 10, T, last note is a; changed by analogy with mm. 61-62.

Le Heurteur, *Souvent*

M. 28, beat 4-m. 29, beat 1, S reads dotted Mi (f') and 2 F's (e', d') in 1536[3]. M. 31, beat 2-m. 32, beat 1, S comprised of SB (g'), SB (f') in 1536[3].

Marle, *Frere Jehan*

M. 7, beat 4-m. 8, beat 1, Ct, tie added by editor. M. 18, note 3-m. 19, note 1, Ct, printed notes f' a' are crossed out and the notes d' b-flat are substituted.

Morel, *Est-il possible*

M. 10, Ct, notes 1-3 appear in coloration in 1538[11]. M. 20, beat 4-m. 21, beat 2, Ct reads SB (f'), Mi (f') in 1538[11]. M. 23, Ct, note 1 replaced by SB (e') and Mi-rest in 1538[11]. Mm. 29ff., Ct and T, text setting used in the transcription is taken from 1538[11].

Senterre, *Faict-elle pas*

M. 15, Ct reads SB, dotted Mi, SM in 1538[10].

Villiers, *Cueur sans mercy*

M. 9, S, note 2 is replaced by a dotted Mi (a') and a SM (g') in 1538[16]. M. 16, beat 4-m. 17, beat 1, T, 2 Mi's in place of the SB in 1538[16]. M. 17, S, notes 2-4 replaced by a SB (c'') in 1538[16]. M. 27, S, notes 2 and 3 are both Mi's in 1538[16].

Villiers, *En grant*

M. 8, S, note 2 replaced by dotted Mi (f') and SM (e') in 1538[15]; Ct, note 5 replaced by 2 Mi's (c', c') in 1538[15]. M. 20, S, notes 1-2 replaced by a SB (b-flat) in 1538[15]. M. 20, note 4-m. 21, note 1, S, these notes replaced by a dotted Mi (d') in 1538[15]. M. 31, beat 4-m. 32, beat 1, S, rendered as dotted Mi (f') and SM (e') in 1538[15]. M. 32, Ct, note 1 replaced by 2 Mi's (c', c') in 1538[15].

Villiers, *Est-il*

All text spellings in this edition are from 1540[13]. M. 14, beat 4-m. 15, beat 1, Ct, 2 Mi's in place of the SB (represented here by the tie) in 1540[13]. M. 15, beats 1-2, T, 2 Mi's in place of the SB in 1540[13].

Villiers, *Le dueil*

Text underlay in the transcription taken from 1549[17]. M. 8, S, notes 2-3 are replaced by a SB (g') in 1549[17]. M. 9, T, notes 1 and 2 replaced by a SB in 1549[17]; all voices, last note is a Br in 1549[17]. M. 17, note 4-m. 18, note 1, S consists of Mi (a'), SM (a') in place of the dotted Mi (represented here by the tie) in 1549[17]. M. 18, beat 3-m. 19, beat 1, S, this passage reads Mi (d'), Mi (f'), Mi (f') in 1549[17]. M. 26, T, beat 2 comprised of SM (g), SM (f) in 1549[17].

Villiers, *Rien*

Mm. 10-14, Ct, text setting in this section taken from 1543[11] and 1543[12]. M. 13, T, note 6 is replaced by 2 Mi's in 1543[11/12]. M. 31, beat 4-m. 32, beat 1, S, these beats comprised of a dotted Mi (a') and 2 F's (g', f') in 1543[11/12].

Villiers, *Tristesse*

M. 5, T, beat 4 comprised of SM (b-flat) and 2 F's (a, g) in 1539[20]. M. 23, S, notes 3-5 replaced by SB (a') in 1539[20].

Fresneau or Senterre, *Thenot*

M. 10, Ct, notes 3-4 replaced by a dotted Mi (c') and a SM (b-flat) in 1544[9]. M. 23, Ct, beats 3-4 comprised of 4 SM's (a, a, b-flat, c') in 1544[9]. M. 34, S, note 1 replaced by 2 SM's in 1545[11]. M. 36, T, note 3 replaced by a dotted Mi (d') and SM (c') in 1544[9]. M. 37, Ct, note 1 replaced by a dotted Mi (d') and 2 F's (c', d'), in 1544[9]. M. 40, T, note 2 replaced by 2 F's (c', c') in 1544[9]. M. 41, Ct, notes 1-2 replaced by a Mi (c') in 1544[9]. M. 42, beat 4-m. 43, beat 2, Ct, these notes replaced by a dotted Mi (f') and 3 SM's (e', e', d') in 1544[9]. M. 48, Ct part comprised of Mi-rest, Mi (f'), and 4 SM's (all f') in 1544[9].

## Acknowledgments

The editor would like to acknowledge the invaluable assistance of Drs. Imogene Horsley, Albert Cohen, and William Mahrt of Stanford University; Dr. Howard M. Brown of the University of Chicago; and Dr. Lawrence Bernstein of the University of Pennsylvania. Special thanks are also due to Dr. Daniel Heartz of the University of California at Berkeley for the use of his microfilm collection of Attaingnant prints.

Leta E. Miller

July 1981                    Santa Cruz, California

# Notes

1. Lawrence Bernstein, "The 'Parisian Chanson': Problems of Style and Terminology," *Journal of the American Musicological Society* 31, no. 2 (1978): 237-240.

2. Ibid., and Leta E. Miller, "The Chansons of French Provincial Composers, 1530-1550: A Study of Stylistic Trends" (Ph.D. diss., Stanford University, 1978).

3. Almost all of the chansons by the provincial composers are à 4. The current study does not deal with two- and three-voice compositions.

4. The works of three other composers, Simon Magdelain, Eustorg de Beaulieu, and Clément Janequin, are already available in modern editions. Sources for the first two are listed in Miller, "The Chansons of French Provincial Composers," 1: 217 ff. Janequin's works are published in A. Tillman Merritt and François Lesure, eds., *Clément Janequin, Chansons Polyphoniques* (Monaco: Éditions de l'Oiseau-Lyre, 1965).

5. Although du Verdier (*Les bibliothèques Françoises de La Croix du Maine et de du Verdier*) claims that there were eighteen volumes in the *Parangon* series, historical records document the publication of only eleven. See Samuel F. Pogue, *Jacques Moderne* (Geneva: Librairie Droz, 1969), p. 18.

6. For reference to Cadéac, see F. Lesure and G. Thibault, "Bibliographie des éditions musicales publiées par Nicolas du Chemin (1549-1576)," *Annales Musicologiques* I (1953): 316 (no. 48). For reference to Colin, see ibid., nos. 8 and 49-51, and Pogue, *Jacques Moderne*, pp. 206-207 (no. 60-61). The reference to Marle may be found in Lesure and Thibault, "Du Chemin," p. 338 (no. 89).

7. See William Lengefeld, "The Motets of Pierre Colin" (Ph.D. diss., University of Iowa, 1969), p. 13; *Die Musik in Geschichte und Gegenwart* (Kassel, 1957), s.v. "Cadéac, Pierre," by Nanie Bridgman; and Stanley Sadie, ed., *The New Grove Dictionary of Music and Musicians* (1980), s.v. "Cadéac, Pierre," by Lawrence Bernstein, and s.v. "Colin, Pierre," by W. Chris Lengefeld.

8. G. Desjardins, *Histoire de la Cathédrale de Beauvais* (Beauvais, 1865), pp. 75 and 120.

9. A. R. Collette and A. Bourdon, *Histoire de la maîtrise de Rouen* (1892), p. 115 and Appendix, p. 5.

10. Ibid., pp. 115-116: "On se plaignait qu'ils n'étaient pas suffisamment instruits, . . . qu'ils s'acquittaient mal de leurs fonctions, ne connaissant pas bien les cérémonies, . . .

qu'ils manquaient de gravité et de retenue jusque dans le choeur, . . . qu'ils sortaient de la maîtrise sans permission pour s'en aller par la ville réciter *des comédies. . . .*"

11. *The New Grove Dictionary of Music and Musicians*, s.v. "Dulot, François," by Courtney Adams.

12. J.-A. Clerval, *L'ancienne maîtrise de Notre-Dame de Chartres du Vᵉ siècle à la révolution* (1899), pp. 81 and 293; *Die Musik in Geschichte und Gegenwart*, s.v. "Guyon, Jean," by F. Lesure; and *The New Grove Dictionary of Music and Musicians*, s.v. "Guyon, Jean," by Caroline Cunningham.

13. Clerval, *L'ancienne maîtrise de Notre-Dame de Chartres*, p. 81, and François Lesure, "Some Minor French Composers of the Sixteenth Century," in *Aspects of Medieval and Renaissance Music*, ed. Jan La Rue (New York: W. W. Norton, 1966), p. 543.

14. Lesure, "Some Minor French Composers," pp. 538-539.

15. Ibid., pp. 543 and 544.

16. *Die Musik in Geschichte und Gegenwart*, s.v. "Le Heurteur, Guillaume," by Edith Weber, and *The New Grove Dictionary of Music and Musicians*, s.v. "Le Heurteur, Guillaume," by Lawrence Bernstein.

17. For more detailed biographical information, see Frank Dobbins, "The Chanson at Lyons in the Sixteenth Century" (Ph.D. diss., Oxford University, 1972). Dr. Dobbins presents transcriptions of all of the chansons of Coste, and of selected works by Fresneau and Villiers.

Additional chansons by these three composers are published in Leta Miller, ed., *Chansons from the French Provinces (1530-1550), Vol. 1: Lyon* (Berkeley: Musica Sacra et Profana, 1980).

18. *A bien compter* was published in 1538 and 1540 by Attaingnant, and in 1538 by Moderne. (See RISM 1538[12], 1538[17], and 1540[10].) Three other works ascribed to Fresneau by Moderne are given to Senterre or Janequin by Attaingnant.

19. These three are *Montez soubdain, Ung Jacobin*, and *Ung Cordelier*.

20. This collection is primarily a re-edition of the *Musica Nova* of 1540, probably published by Andrea Arrivabene. See H. Colin Slim, ed., *Musica nova accommodata per cantar et sonar sopra organi*, Monuments of Renaissance Music, vol. 1 (Chicago and London: University of Chicago Press, 1964).

Coste's piece, however, appears only in Moderne's edition. See Pogue, *Jacques Moderne*, pp. 182-184; Pogue dates this work as coming from 1544, although Slim and RISM place it later.

21. Although the composer's name appears in this form in the index of Moderne's collection, it is printed as "G. Coste" above the music itself. For further information on Coste, see Pogue, *Jacques Moderne*, pp. 25, 60, and 67, and Dobbins, "The Chanson at Lyons," pp. 144 and 174.

22. Pogue, *Jacques Moderne*, pp. 321 ff. (and especially p. 341).

23. For a modern edition of this work, see Pogue, *Jacques Moderne*, pp. 387-389.

24. In the second stanza of this text, there are annotations that refer to Aneau, Lyons, and Villiers. See Dobbins, "The Chanson at Lyons," p. 65.

25. The poem, with a translation, may be found in Pogue, *Jacques Moderne*, p. 65.

26. Ibid., p. 41, and Dobbins, "The Chanson at Lyons," p. 143.

27. The sixteen works include: 1 by Fresneau; 1 by Villiers; 2 by Marle; 2 by Morel; 2 by Samin; 5 by Senterre; and 3 by Godard (2 *à* 4 and 1 *à* 5).

28. Miller, "The Chansons of French Provincial Composers."

29. The sample of provincial chansons included approximately half of the works of each master and encompassed the entire chronological period during which each composer's chansons appeared in print. Janequin's works were not included in the provincial sample, but were treated separately (see Miller, "The Chansons of French Provincial Composers," ch. 7). The sample of Parisian chansons was selected to accurately represent the style of the majority of works published during a particular year by each composer. For further details on the selection of the samples, see Miller, "The Chansons of French Provincial Composers," pp. 79-80 and 184-189.

30. Bernstein, "The 'Parisian Chanson,' " p. 226.

31. For example, in Gustave Reese, *Music in the Renaissance* (New York: W. W. Norton, 1959), pp. 292 and 293.

32. *Harvard Dictionary of Music*, s.v. "Notes"; Sébastien de Brossard, *Dictionnaire de Musique* (Paris: Ballard, 1703), s.v. "Pausa."

33. For the detailed statistics, see Miller, "The Chansons of French Provincial Composers," pp. 165-166.

34. In some of Janequin's early works, the musical form is related to the text form; many are through-composed. Even in his later chansons, where the tripartite form is common, Janequin often introduced musical variants in repeated sections or altered the common text line distribution.

35. An exception to this practice occurred with Villiers' *Le dueil issu*, where there were compelling reasons for selecting the earlier edition. Later reprints by Du Chemin, Le Roy et Ballard, Phalèse, et al., of chansons that first appeared in Attaingnant or Moderne collections were not used in preparing this edition.

36. Daniel Heartz, *Pierre Attaingnant, Royal Printer of Music: A Historical Study and Bibliographical Catalogue* (Berkeley and Los Angeles: University of California Press, 1969), p. 148, and Pogue, *Jacques Moderne*, p. 53.

# Chronological Index
# of Chansons

# Texts and Translations

(Translations by Leta Miller and Rebecca Harris-Warrick)

*Soyez seur que la repentence* (Jean Bastard)

Soyez seur que la repentence
Suyvoit de bien pres le peché
D'avoir intermis l'aliance
Qui noz cueurs avoit attaché.
Helas, j'en ay le cueur fasché,
Et si ne scay aucun moyen
Pour monstrer mon cueur estre tien
Sinon en disant quand je y pense:
"Helas, amy, je congnois bien
Que ne puis nyer mon offence."

(You may be sure that repentance
Followed closely after the sin
Of having broken the alliance
That had·bound our hearts.
Alas, my heart grieves over it,
And thus I know no means
Of showing that my heart is yours
Except by saying, whenever I think of it:
"Alas, love, I know well
That I cannot deny my offense.")

*Amour et moy* (Pierre Cadéac)

Amour et moy avons faict une dame
Voulans ouyr les plaintes d'amytié.
Dont j'ay vaincu le corps et amour l'ame,
Et converty sa rigueur en pityé.

(Love and I have made a woman
Wish to hear the sighs of affection.
I conquered her body and love, her soul,
And changed her severity into pity.)

*En languissant* (Pierre Cadéac)

En languissant je consomme mes jours.
Jour et nuyt suys en attendant secours.
Cours vistement allegeance m'amye
Me secourir car d'aultre n'ay envye,
Ou a la mort je vois plus que le cours.

(I consume my days in languishing.
Day and night I await relief.
My love, have solace; run quickly
To help me because I desire no other,
Or I will go racing toward death.)

*Comment, mon coeur* (Pierre Colin)

Comment, mon coeur, es-tu donc dispensé
De te donner sans de moy conger prendre?
Et vous, mes yeulx, vous avez commencé
Sans vous pouvoir aulcunement defendre.
Par voz fins tours, me contraingnez d'apprendre
Que c'est d'aymer sans espoir d'avoir mieulx.
O coeur lassif, o impudiques yeulx,
Qui tant courez et estes tant volages,
C'est bien raison que soyez douloureux,
Puis qu'avez faict vous mesme le message.

(How, my heart, did you thus proceed
To surrender yourself without my permission?
And you, my eyes, you started out
Without being able to defend yourselves in any way.
By your devious tricks you compel me to learn
What it is to love without hope of having more.
O lascivious heart, o unchaste eyes,
You who run so much and are so fickle,
There is a good reason for you to be sorrowful,
Since you yourselves have played the messenger.)

*Si les oyseaulx* (Gabriel Coste)

Si les oyseaulx n'avoyent espoyr
Sortir des caiges quelque jour,
Ilz ne pourroyent sans mourir voyr
Vouler les aultres a l'entour.
Ainsi l'espoyr de vostre amour
Me nourrit en captivité,
Et y vouldrois faire retour,
Quant bien j'en serois deicté.

(If the birds had no hope
Of leaving their cages some day,
They would not be able to watch, without dying,
The others flying [freely] all around.
Thus the hope of your love
Nourishes me in captivity,
And there I would wish to return,
Even if I were led out from there.)

*Ung pouvre aymant* (Gabriel Coste)

Ung pouvre aymant de l'amour mesdisoit,
Estant blessé sans y scavoir remede.
Pourquoy son cueur ce lieu la eslisoit,

Quant avec soy en liberté vivoit?
Il est cruel et la personne laide.[1]

(A poor lover spoke ill of love,
Having been wounded without knowing a remedy.
Why did his heart choose that place [for love],
When it had lived with him in liberty?
It [the heart] is cruel and the beloved, ugly.)[1]

*Combien que j'ay*                    (Jean Doublet)

Combien que j'ay douleur vehemente,
Je ne me veulx de t'aymer repentir.
Donque de brief fais-moy ce bien sentir,
Affin qu'ailleurs mon corps ne mecte en vente.

(No matter how violent my suffering,
I do not wish to repent loving you.
Therefore let me experience this pleasure soon,
So that I don't have to put my body up for sale
    elsewhere.)

*En esperant*                    (François Dulot)

En esperant le printemps advenir,
Tout raverdit a la saison nouvelle.
Il n'est dur cueur qui ne se renouvelle,
S'il n'est surpris d'amoureux souvenir.

(Expecting spring to arrive,
Everything turns green in the new season.
There is no hardened heart which is not renewed,
If it is surprised by an amorous memory.)

*Mignons qui suivés la rote*            (Henry Fresneau)

Mignons qui suivés la rote
Du dieu d'amours, vray heritiers,
Donnez pour faire une marotte
A ces faulx jaloux vieulx rotiers.
Venez les veoir tost a milliers.
Ne frappez a la porte,
Ilz sont registrez au papier
Greffé de Mere Sotte.[2]

(My dears, who follow the route
Of the god of love, [his] true heirs,
Give [money] to these false, jealous old travelers
So that they can put on a play.
Come soon by the thousands to see them.
Don't knock on the door;
They are enrolled on the official paper
Of Mère Sotte.)[2]

*Oeil importum*                    (Henry Fresneau)

Oeil importum qui mon cueur a rendu
Digne de veoir que grande est son offence,
Cesse ta force; amour m'a deffendu
Pour l'advenir son heureuse acointance.

Vivraige donc sans avoir esperance
De recouvrir le moyen d'amytié?
Non, car j'auray si triste repentance,
Que je feray a quelqu'une pitié.

(Unwelcome eye, who rendered my heart
Worthy of seeing how great is its offense,
Cease your force; love has denied me
The happiness of its acquaintance in the future.
Will I thus live without having hope
Of recovering the means of love?
No, because my repentance will be sad enough
To create pity in some lady.)

*Souspir d'amours*                    (Henry Fresneau)

Souspir d'amours, pensée de plaisir,
Qui de m'amye me donnez l'esperance,
Donne a mon vueil telle resjouyssance
Qu'a tousjours mais ne me puisse finir.

(Sigh of love, thought of pleasure,
You who give me hope of [success with] my
    beloved,
Please grant me such rejoicing
That it might never end for me.)

*Longtemps y a*                    (Robert Godard)

Longtemps y a que langueur et tristesse,
Doeul et ennuy ont visité mon cueur,
Et ce que plus le tormente et oppresse,
C'est ung desir qui le tient en vigueur.
Mais bon espoir, voulant estre vainqueur,
Ne peult souffrir qui tombe en tel martire.
"Resjouy-toy," dict-il, "car la rigueur
Te donnera trop plus que ne desire."

(For a long time languor and sadness,
Grief and worry have visited my heart;
And what torments and oppresses it still more
Is a desire which grips it forcefully.
But good hope, wishing to be the conqueror,
Cannot put up with one who falls into such
    martyrdom.
"Rejoice," he says, "because this harshness
Will give you much more than you can possibly
    desire.")

*Mariez-moy mon pere*                    (Robert Godard)

Mariez-moy mon pere.
    Il est temps ou jamais.
Ou si vous ne le faictes,
    Contraincte je seray
De vous dire en deux motz,
    Ma volunté feray.
Et fault que je le face,
    Cela je vous prometz.

(Marry me off, father.
  It's now or never.
Or if you don't do it,
  I will be compelled
To tell you in no uncertain terms
  That I shall have my will.
And it is necessary that I do it;
  This I promise you.)

*De noz deux cueurs*                    (Jean Guyon)

De noz deux cueurs soit seulle volunté,
Et le vouloir, vray semblant de beaulté,
Maintien en luy mutuelle allegeance,
Sans convertir le plaisir en souffrance
Qu'amour nous a pour loyer presenté.

(Of our two hearts let there be only one will,
And may desire, the true semblance of beauty,
Maintain in itself mutual solace,
Without converting pleasure into the suffering
Which love has demanded from us in payment.)

*Gaultier rancontra Janeton*           (Jean Guyon)

Gaultier rancontra Janeton,
Qui luy sembla coincte et jolye.
En luy maniant le teton,
S'efforça faire la folye.
Elle, qui de melencolye
Mouroit par faulte de cela,
Luy dict, "Mon amy, je te prye,
Faiz le moy preste, me voila."

(Gaultier chanced upon Janeton,
Who seemed charming and pretty to him.
While handling her breast,
He tried to make advances.
She, who was dying of melancholy
For lack of this,
Said to him, "My love, I pray you,
Do it to me quickly; here I am.")

*Doeul, double doeul*     (Nicolle des Celliers d'Hesdin)

Doeul, double doeul, renfort de desplaisir,
Tristesse, ennuy, ennemys de plaisir,
De ma langueur prenez solicitude,
Et de mon mal voyant l'amaritude,
Ne me donnez de vivre plus loysir.

(Grief, double grief, reinforcement of displeasure,
Sadness, worry, enemies of pleasure,
Be solicitous of my languor,
And seeing the bitterness of my pain,
Don't give me any more time to live.)

*Ce moys de may*                  (Jean Le Bouteiller)

Ce moys de may au joly vert bosquet,
C'est ung plaisir que d'estre soubz l'ombrage.

L'ung faict chapeaux, l'aultre faict ung bouquet,
Ce moys de may au joly vert bosquet.
Tout cueur fasché lors reprent son courage.
Le rossignol en son plaisant langaige
Faict rage au boscage, son chant ramage
Triumphe assis sur la fleur du muguet,
Ce moys de may au joly vert bosquet.

(In May in the pretty green wood,
It is a pleasure to be under the shade of the trees.
One person is making hats, another a bouquet,
In May in the pretty green wood.
Every angry heart takes courage.
The nightingale, in its pleasing language,
Makes a racket in the wood [with] its warbling song;
It triumphs [while] seated on the lily of the valley,
In May in the pretty green wood.)

*Ma dame ung jour*        (Guillaume Le Heurteur)

Ma dame ung jour doulx baiser me donna,
Et me promist que j'auroys la sequelle,
Mais tost aprez elle m'abandonna,
Pour ung nouveau qui fut amoureux d'elle.

(My lady gave me a sweet kiss one day,
And promised me that I would have the sequel,
But soon after, she abandoned me
For a new one who was in love with her.)

*Or my rendez mon karolus*[3]  (Guillaume Le Heurteur)

  *Or my rendez mon karolus*
  *Tant belle jeune fille,*
  *Or my rendez mon karolus,*
  *N'en parlez plus.*

Mon pere avoit ung jardinet,
Couvert de rose et de muguet,
  *Or my rendez . . .*

Le filz du roy sy umbrageoit;
Une tant belle amye avoit,
  *Or my rendez . . .*

Toutes les foys que la baisoit,
La povre fille si trembloit,
  *Or my rendez . . .*

  (*Now give me back my carolus*
  *Lovely young girl,*
  *Now give me back my carolus;*
  *Don't speak of it any more.*

My father had a little garden,
Covered with roses and lilies of the valley.
  *Now give me . . .*

The king's son took the shade there;
He had such a beautiful friend.
  *Now give me . . .*

Every time he kissed her,
The poor girl trembled.
   *Now give me . . .* )

*Souvent amour*                     (Guillaume Le Heurteur)

Souvent amour me livre grant torment,
Mais je congnois qu'il est traitre parfaict;
Parquoy je veulx dissimuler son faict,
Pour en avoir meilleur contentement.

(Love often gives me great torment,
But I know that he is a perfect traitor;
Because of this I wish to conceal his work,
In order to derive more contentment from it.)

*Frere Jehan fust ung jour surprins*   (Nicolas de Marle)

Frere Jehan fust ung jour surprins
Avec une garse couché.
Dont fut en chapitre reprins,
Et a ung pillier attaché.
Puis Dieu scait comment esmouché,
Criant tousjours, "Frere tout beau,
Si pour chascun forfaict nouveau,
Vous me vouliez ainsi houssé,
Je puis bien dire adieu ma peau,
Car je ne m'en scauroys passé."

(Brother John was surprised one day
While lying with a young girl.
For this he was taken back to the chapter
And tied to a pillar.
Then God knows how he was beaten,
Crying always, "Dear brother,
If for each new crime,
You wish me thus to be 'dusted,'
I may as well say farewell to my skin,
Because I wouldn't know how to give up [these
   crimes].")

*L'enfant Amour*                     (Nicolas de Marle;
                                     text by Clément Marot)

L'enfant Amour n'a plus son arc estrange,
Dont il blessoit d'hommes et cueurs et testes.
Avec celuy de Diane faict change,
Dont elle alloit aux champs faire les questes.
Ilz ont changé, n'en faictes plus d'enquestes,
Et si on dict, "A quoy le congnois-tu?"
Je voy qu'Amour chasse souvent aux bestes,
Et qu'elle attainct les hommes de vertu.

(Cupid no longer has his strange bow,
With which he wounded both the hearts and minds
   of men.
He is exchanging it for Diana's,
Which she took into the fields for hunting.
They have made the exchange, I can assure you,
And if someone asks, "How do you know that?"

I can see that Cupid often hunts beasts,
And that she [Diana] is wounding men of virtue.)

*Est-il possible*                     (Clément Morel)

Est-il possible que l'on puisse trouver
Aulcun moyen pour avoir vostre grace?
Qu'en dictes-vous? En pourroit-on finer?
Dictes ouy ou mon cueur se trespasse.

(Is it possible for one to find
Any way of obtaining your grace?
What do you say? Could we put an end to this?
Say yes, or my heart will die.)

*Plaisir n'ay plus*                     (Clément Morel;
                                        text by Clément Marot)

Plaisir n'ay plus mais vis en desconfort.
Fortune m'a remis en grant douleur.
L'heur que j'avois s'est tourné en malheur.
Malheureux est qui n'a aucun confort.

(I no longer have pleasure, but live in misery.
Fortune has set me back into great sorrow.
The happiness I had has turned into unhappiness.
Unhappy is he who has no comfort.)

*Amour m'a mis*                     (Vulfran Samin)

Amour m'a mis en si grand desconfort
Par le pourchas de trop mauldicte envie,
Qu'autant que vois de moy fouir la mort,
Autant me veulx eslongner de la vie.

(Love has placed me in such great misery
Through the pursuit of so much accursed longing,
That as much as I see death fleeing from me,
That much do I wish to withdraw from life.)

*Comment, mon cueur*                     (Vulfran Samin)

Comment, mon cueur, es-tu donc dispensé
De te donner sans de moy congé prendre?
Et vous, mes yeulx, vous avez commencé
Sans vous pouvoir aulcunement deffendre.
Par voz fins tours me contraignes d'apprendre
Que c'est d'aymer sans espoir d'avoir mieulx
O cueur lascif, o impudicques yeulx,
Qui tant courez et estes tant volaiges,
C'est bien raison que soyez doloreux,
Puis qu'avez faict vous mesme le mesaige.

(For translation, see above, Colin, *Comment, mon coeur*)

*Faict-elle pas bien*                     (Pierre Senterre)

Faict-elle pas bien
D'aymer qui luy donne?
Elle est belle et bonne,
Et si ne vault rien.

Elle ayme le mien,
Non pas ma personne,
Et si s'abandonne,
A qui luy dict, "Tient."

(Does she not do well
To love whoever gives her [gifts]?
She is beautiful and good,
Even if she is worth nothing.
She loves my money,
Not my person,
And thus she abandons herself
To whoever says to her, "Take this.")

*Autant que moy*                    (Pierre de Villiers)

Autant que moy heureuse pourrez estre,
Si mon amour voulez au vray choisir,
Et en souffrant vous le pourrez congnoistre,
Sans recepvoir en aymant desplaisir.
Le bien sera donc esgal au desir,
Trouvant l'amour en ses faictz honorable.
Estant honneur joinct a nostre plaisir,
Noz cueurs vivront en fermeté louable.

(You will be as happy as I
If you want to truly choose my love,
And by permitting [this], you will be able to
    experience [my love],
Without receiving displeasure in loving.
Goodness will thus be equal to desire,
Finding love honorable in his actions.
Having joined honor to our pleasure,
Our hearts will live in laudable steadfastness.)

*Cueur sans mercy*                    (Pierre de Villiers)

Cueur sans mercy, yeulx meurtriers de ma joye,
Beauté sans foy, gay maintien sans doulceur,
Ma face soit miroer de ta rigueur,
Et mes souspirs pour tesmoings je t'envoye.

(Heart without mercy, eyes—murderers of my joy,
Beauty without faith, gay appearance without
    sweetness,
Let my face be a mirror of your severity,
And I send you my sighs as witnesses.)

*Elle est m'amye*                    (Pierre de Villiers)

Elle est m'amye, en parle qui parler vouldra.
Son doulx recueil mon pouvre cueur point.
Mais si je puis parvenir a mon point,
J'en jouiray ou espoir my fauldra.

(She is my love; let people say what they will.
Her sweet appearance pierces my poor heart.

But if I am able to attain my goal,
I will delight in it, or I will need [the aid of] hope.)

*En grant douleur*                    (Pierre de Villiers)

En grant douleur faict son triste demeure,
Mon pauvre cueur bany de son plaisir,
N'ayant sinon de soy trister desir,
En attendant l'attente que je meure.

(My poor heart, banished from its pleasure,
Makes its sad abode in great suffering,
Having nothing but the desire to grieve,
While waiting in the expectation of my death.)

*Est-il ung mal*                    (Pierre de Villiers)

Est-il ung mal si rigoureux au monde
Que de sa dame ung doulx propos ouyr,
Si le congé de par elle se fonde
Pour son amant secretement fouyr?
Las, quel durté, quel fascheux resjouyr,
Quant ung tel faindre avec amour converse,
Dissimulant pour estre part adverse
De ce que bouche appelloit amoureux.
O quel semblant pour causer controverse.
Est-il au monde ung mal si rigoureux?

(Is there any pain in the world so severe
As to hear a sweet remark from one's lady
When she has decided to take her leave
In order to secretly flee from her lover?
Alas, what harshness, what distressing rejoicing,
When such a sham resides with love,
Dissembling, in order to oppose
What the mouth used to call love.
Oh, what a pretense for causing dispute.
Is there any pain in the world so severe?)

*Le dueil issu*                    (Pierre de Villiers)

Le dueil issu de la joye incertaine
Permet aux yeulx seullement le plourer.
De l'endurer donc vous aurez la peine
Avec celuy qui vous peult demourer.
O quel malheur a voulu procurer
Qu'ayez perdu au change pour choisir.
C'est double dueil que vous fault endurer,
Si mon travail vous peult donner plaisir.

(The grief resulting from uncertain joy
Only permits the eyes to weep.
Thus you will have the pain of enduring it
With the one who remains with you.
Oh, what misfortune determined
That you would lose in exchange for choosing.
It is a double grief that you must endure,
If my work can give you pleasure.)

*Rien n'est plus cher* (Pierre de Villiers;
text by Charles de Sainte-Marthe)

Rien n'est plus cher que ce que l'on desire,
Et moins on l'a plus on y est ardant.
Lors qu'on ne peulx a son souhait suffire,
Le desir croist tousjours en attendant.
Quant aulcun est de jouir pretendant,
Par un espoir a demi se contente,
Et s'il advient que fortune presente
Contentement de la chose attendue,
En jouissant du fruict de son attente,
Le desir cesse et l'amour continue.

(Nothing is dearer than that which one desires,
And the less one has it, the more one burns for it.
When one is not worthy of his wish,
The desire [for it] increases continually while he waits.
When someone aspires to joy,
He half satisfies himself with a hope,
And if it happens that good fortune presents
Contentment from the awaited thing,
While enjoying the fruit of his waiting,
Desire ceases and love continues.)

*Tristesse, ennuy* (Pierre de Villiers)

Tristesse, ennuy, douleur, melancholye,
Peine et regret, ennemys de jeunesse,
Tiennent mon cueur, et desespoir le lye,
Pour mettre a fin ma vie en grand destresse.
Dame pourtant si une telle oppresse
Mue le teint a ma piteuse face,
Ne t'esbays, mais bien la cause adresse
A ta rigueur et non pas a ta grace.

(Sadness, ennui, sorrow, melancholy,
Pain and regret, enemies of youth,
[All] hold my heart, and despair binds it
In order to bring my distressing life to an end.
Nevertheless, lady, if such oppression
Changes the color in my piteous face,
Do not be amazed, but attribute the cause
To your rigor, and not to your grace.)

*Thenot estoit* (Pierre Senterre or Henry Fresneau)

Thenot estoit en son cloz resjouy,
Qui regardoit les bourgeons profiter.
Catin avoit devers le cloz ouy
Le rossignol sur l'aubepin chanter.
Au cloz entra, puis s'en alla tanter
Le bon Thenot du combat amoureux.
"Helas, Catin, l'instrument vigoreulx
N'ay plus ainsy que l'avoys en ma force."
"Bon cueur, Thenot, en ce combat heureulx,
Le bon cheval jamais ne devient rosse."

(Thenot was enjoying his garden,
Watching the buds grow.
Catin heard, near the garden,
The nightingale singing in the hawthorne.
She entered the garden and began to tempt
Good Thenot into amorous combat.
"Alas, Catin, I no longer have the vigorous
    instrument
Which I once had in my power."
"Take heart, Thenot, in this happy combat,
The good horse never becomes an old nag.")

# Notes to the Texts and Translations

1. Alternately, "la personne l'aide," i.e, "the person [of love] aids it."

2. This text is apparently a promotional advertisement for a traveling theater company. "In the fifteenth century . . . in various large towns of the North . . . companies of *fous* or *sots* were formed under the direction of a *prince*, of a *mère sotte* or of.a *mère folle*. The *sots* of Paris were called *les Enfants Sans-Souci*, and garbed in green and yellow motley, with bells and asses' ears on their caps, they entertained the populace with their pleasantries, which generally took the form of the *Sotie*, a short satirical piece more often than not political in tone, attacking the King, the Government, the nobility, or the Church." (See Kathleen T. Butler, *A History of French Literature* [London: Methuen and Co., 1923], pp. 76-77). The most famous *Mère Sotte* was Pierre Gringore (ca. 1470-1539). A *marrotte* is a fool's sceptor; here it has been translated freely as a "play."

See also Howard Mayer Brown, *Music in the French Secular Theater, 1400-1550* (Cambridge: Harvard University Press, 1963), pp. 29-30, and *The New Grove Dictionary of Music and Musicians*, s.v. "Fresneau, Henry," by Frank Dobbins. The editor would also like to acknowledge the help of Dr. Leonard Johnson, Department of French, University of California at Berkeley.

3. A carolus is a copper or nickel coin issued under Charles VIII.

Plate I.    Superius and tenor parts of Pierre de Villiers' *Elle est m'amye* with the canonic rubric.
From *Le Parangon des Chansons. Second livre . . .* (Lyon: Jacques Moderne, 1538).
By permission of the British Library.

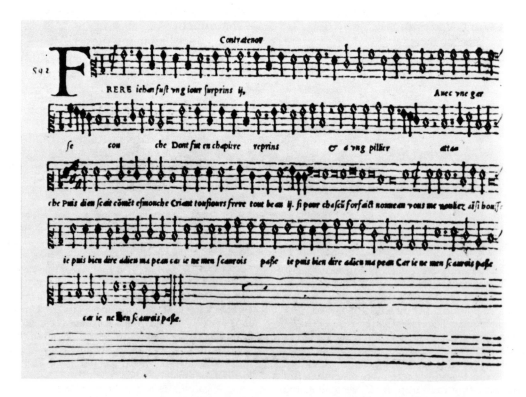

Plate II.    Contratenor part of Nicolas de Marle's *Frere Jehan*,
from the *Trente cincquiesme livre contenant xxiiii chansons nouvelles . . .* (Paris: Pierre Attaingnant, 1549).
By permission of the Bayerische Staatsbibliothek of Munich.

# THIRTY-SIX CHANSONS
# BY FRENCH PROVINCIAL COMPOSERS
## (1529–1550)

# Soyez seur que la repentence

[Jean] Bastard

# Amour et moy

[Pierre] Cadéac

# En languissant

[Pierre] Cadéac

# Comment, mon coeur

P[ierre] Colin

# Si les oyseaulx

G[abriel] Coste

# Ung pouvre aymant

G[abriel] Coste

# Combien que j'ay

[Jean] Doublet

16

# En esperant

[François] Dulot

## Mignons qui suivés la rote

H[enry] Fresneau

20

# Oeil importum

[Henry] Fresneau

-tié? Non, car j'au- ray si tris- te re- pen- tan- ce,
-tié? Non, car j'au- ray si tris- te re- pen- tan- ce,
-tié? Non, car j'au- ray si tris- te re- pen- tan- ce,
Non, car j'au- ray si tris- te re- pen- tan- ce,

Que je fe- ray a quel- qu'u- ne pi- tié.
Que je fe- ray, que je fe- ray a quel- qu'u- ne pi- tié.
Que je fe- ray, [que je fe- ray] a quel- qu'u- ne pi- tié.
Que je fe- ray, [que je fe- ray] a quel- qu'u- ne pi- tié.

# Souspir d'amours

H[enry] Fresneau

Superius
Sous- pir d'a- mours, sous- pir d'a- mours, sous-

Altus
Sous- pir d'a- mours, sous- pir d'a- mours, sous-

Tenor
Sous- pir d'a- mours, sous- pir d'a-

Bassus
Sous- pir d'a- mours, sous- pir d'a-

-le res- jou- ys- san- ce Qu'a tous- jours mais,_____ qu'a tous- jours
_ res- jou- ys- -san- ce Qu'a tous- jours mais_____
-jou- ys- san- -ce Qu'a tous- jours mais, qu'a tous- jours mais ne
-le res- jou- ys- san- -ce Qu'a tous- jours mais, qu'a tous- jours

mais ne me_____ puis- -se fi- - nir. Qu'a nir.
_ ne me puis- se fi- - nir. Qu'a nir.
me puis- - - se fi- nir. Qu'a nir.
mais_____ ne me puis- se, ne me_____ puis- se fi- nir. Qu'a nir.

# Longtemps y a

[Robert] Godard

Superius

Long- -temps y a que lan- gueur

Contratenor

Long- -temps y a que

Tenor

Long- temps y_____ a que lan- gueur et_____

Bassus

Long- temps y a, long- temps y

28

# Mariez-moy mon pere

[Robert] Godard

30

# De noz deux cueurs

[Jean] Guyon

32

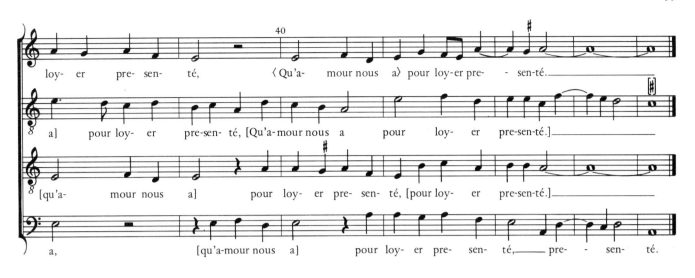

loy- er pre- sen- té, ⟨Qu'a- mour nous a⟩ pour loy-er pre- - sen-té.

a] pour loy- er pre- sen- té, [Qu'a-mour nous a pour loy- er pre-sen-té.]

[qu'a- mour nous a] pour loy- er pre- sen- té, [pour loy- er pre-sen-té.]

a, [qu'a-mour nous a] pour loy- er pre- sen- té,— pre- sen- té.

# Gaultier rancontra Janeton

[Jean] Guion [=Guyon]

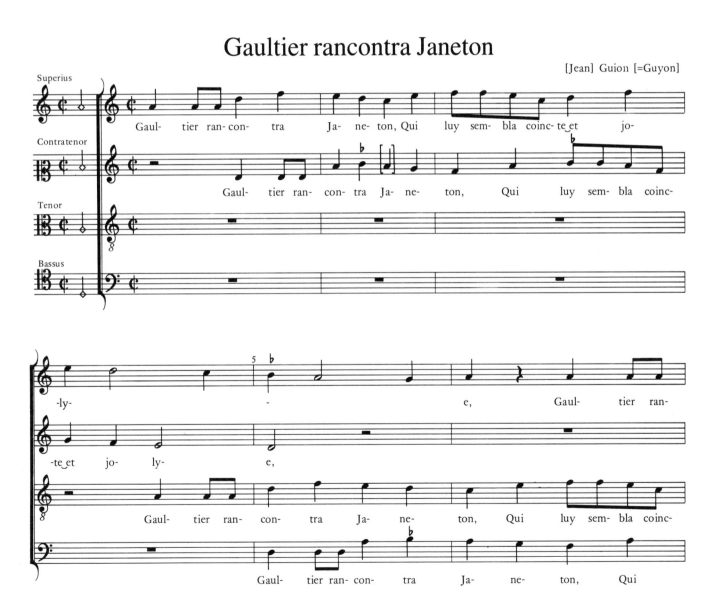

**Superius**
Gaul- tier ran-con- tra Ja- ne- ton, Qui luy sem- bla coinc- te et jo-

**Contratenor**
Gaul- tier ran- con- tra Ja- ne- ton, Qui luy sem- bla coinc-

**Tenor**

**Bassus**

-ly- - e, Gaul- tier ran-

-te et jo- ly- e,

Gaul- tier ran-con- tra Ja- ne- ton, Qui luy sem- bla coinc-

Gaul- tier ran-con- tra Ja- ne- ton, Qui

34

# Doeul, double doeul

[Nicolle des Celliers d'] Hesdin

38

# Ce moys de may

[Jean Le] Bouteiller

42

# Ma dame ung jour

[Guillaume Le] Heurteur

# Or my rendez mon karolus

G[uillaume] Le Heurteur

48

# Souvent amour

[Guillaume Le] Heurteur

# Frere Jehan fust ung jour surprins

[Nicolas] de Marle

# L'enfant Amour

[Text: Clément Marot]

[Nicolas] de Marle

# Est-il possible

[Clément] Morel

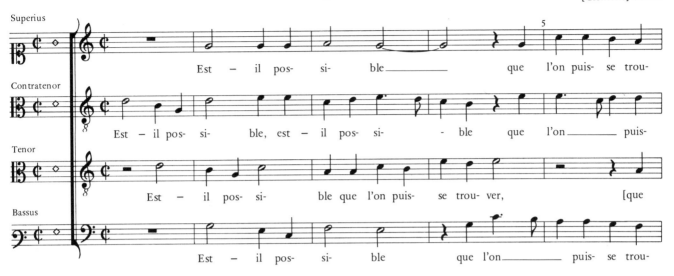

58

# Plaisir n'ay plus

[Text: Clément Marot]

[Clément] Morel

# Amour m'a mis

Vulfran [Samin]

62

# Comment, mon coeur

Vulfran [Samin]

64

## Faict-elle pas bien

[Pierre] Senterre

66

68

# Autant que moy

[Pierre de] Villiers

70

72

# Cueur sans mercy

[Pierre de] Villiers

pour tes- moings je t'en- voy- - e. - e.

je t'en- voy- - - e. Et - e.

-e, pour tes- moings je t'en- voy- e. voy- e.

tes- moings je t'en- voy- e. Et - e.

# Elle est m'amye

Canon: "Qui suyvre me vouldra deux pauses en souspirant pausera."

P[ierre] de Villiers

Superius

El- le est

Altus

El- le est m'a- my-

Tenor

El- le est m'a- my- - e, en par le

Bassus

El- le est, el- le est m'a- my-

El- le est m'a- my- - e, [el- le est

m'a- my- - e, en par le qui par ler

-e, en par le qui par- ler voul-

qui par- ler voul- dra, [en par le qui par- ler voul-

- e, en par le qui par- ler voul- - dra, [en

m'a- my- - e,] en

76

# En grant douleur

[Pierre de] Villiers

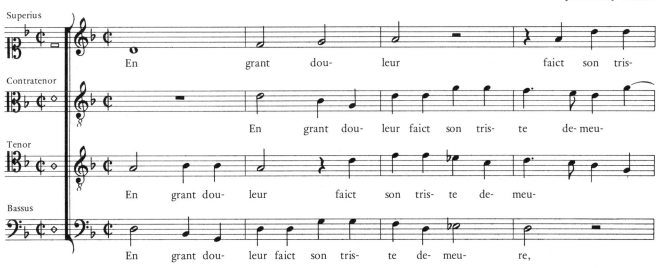

78

# Est-il ung mal

P[ierre] de Villiers

80

# Le dueil issu

P[ierre] de Villiers

82

# Rien n'est plus cher

[Text: Charles de Sainte-Marthe]

[Pierre] de Villiers

84

aul- cun est de jou- ir pre - - tendant,

aul- cun est _____ de jou- ir pre - ten-

aul- cun est de jou- ir pre- ten - - dant, Par un es-

aul- cun est de jou- ir pre - - ten- dant,

Par un _____ es- poir a de- mi

- dant, Par _____ un es- poir a de- mi se

-poir a de- mi se con- ten- te, a de- mi

Par un _____ es- poir a de- mi se con-

se con-ten- - te, Et s'il _____ ad-

con- ten- - te, Et s'il ad- -

se _____ con- ten- te, Et s'il ad- vient,

-ten- - te, Et s'il ad-

-vient que for- tu- ne pre- sen- - - te

-vient que for- tu- ne pre- sen- te Con- ten- - ment

[et s'il ad- vient] que for- tu- ne pre- sen- - te Con-

-vient que for- tu- ne pre- sen- - te Con- ten- te-

85

# Tristesse, ennuy

[Pierre de] Villiers

# Thenot estoit

[Pierre] Senserre [=Senterre]
or H[enry] Fresneau

90